BETTER WAYS TO USE MAPS IN DIGITAL TRANSFORMATION PROJECTS

Why most data integration projects don't work

Karl Jeffery + Dimitris Lyras

January 2020

Published by Software for Domain Experts Ltd

CONTENTS

INTRODUCTION

Why digital enterprise projects fail

Plenty of digital enterprise projects fail. One of the biggest reasons for this could be because there are so many different parts and people which need to come together.

And people all look at what they are doing in different ways, with different sorts of objects relevant to them. One person's objects is not the same as another person's objects.

If we are just dealing with human minds, this is a surmountable problem. The leaders of our ancient armies understood that their view of the world was different to the view of the world of their military leaders, their soldiers, their public, and they could make the system work.

The same for everything else which people have done involving people with different goals, from running ships to schools. Or the relationship between a hairdresser and their customers. People all have different objects which are relevant to them and that doesn't cause any problem.

If there is a common goal, such as winning the war, safe ships, good education, or an effective hairdressing service, people in different roles can see how their activities relate to that goal, and how their various objects and tasks in their work fit with it. People could talk about their work to another person and they would understand each other.

But this does not work when we get computers involved, because computers do not understand goals and activities very well. What computers do understand well is objects. An object can fill a space in a database, or be comprised of a number of database objects (such as a schedule). But objects do not cross easily from one person to another, or one software system (designed for one person) to another.

1

Goals rather than objects

Here's our suggested solution to making digital enterprise projects more successful. People think about their parts of projects more in terms of goals and activities to reach the goals, rather than seeing them as objects. The reason for this is that it is usually easier to align different activities around a common goal, than it is to align objects.

We can draw a map of the different activities which an organisation does to achieve this goal and how they fit together. Then we can use this map as a basis for planning how we want the digital systems to work.

By map, we don't mean a geographical map, but a map as a guide for how the project is working to achieve its goals, which everybody can refer to. Like the way businesspeople talk about roadmaps.

A geographical map is also created to help achieve a goal too, usually, to help someone go somewhere, not just an indication of places in geography.

Our daily life and health – objects or activities?

To try to explain this concept in less abstract terms, let's look at the things we all do in our daily life in order to function, such as eating, sleeping, exercising, dressing, socialising, working.

Are these objects or activities? It really doesn't matter. Our own heads can mix together objects and activities with no problem, and nobody needs to think about how we do these things apart from ourselves.

We might notice that other people take a different approach to these things than we do, even close friends and people we know well from work or socialising. Breakfast for one person is an activity to a goal, breakfast for another is an activity to a different goal, breakfast for another is just an object, or what I do at 8am.

Dog's mess on the street

But here's an example where objects don't map between people and it does cause a problem - your children step in a dog's mess on the pavement. What selfish dog owners did not clean it up?

There are two parties – the parent and the dog owner. Let's look at their "objects". The dog owner should remember to take a plastic bag when they take their dog for a walk. If they forget, or do not have one, and the dog still wants a walk, then they have to work out how else to clean it up - or might be wondering if anyone will notice their dog's mess on the pavement, or fine them.

As a parent you are taking your children for a walk. You keep a look out for dog's mess and encourage them to look out for it themselves. If they are not careful, it comes down to luck.

Dog walk, bag, bag supplies, remembering bag, dog owner attitude, mess. Child walk, teaching, looking, bad luck, messy shoes. These could all be described in data and put in a computer system. But it would be crazy to tie them together into an equation.

We would not make software for this either, but we do make software to manage and track safety, cleanliness, tasks, supplies in store, current supplies, skills, statuses. We often try to integrate different systems together, such as the parent's system and the dog owner's system. Can you see now why it is so hard to make this integration work?

How about instead we focussed on a common goal and what activities led to the achievement of this goal. The goal here could be clean and pleasant streets. The relevant activities are the dog's owner's effort, the parent's effort, the child's steps. We could more easily put this together in a map.

If the dog owner doesn't have a plastic bag, there is a conflicting goal - the dog owner wants the convenience of getting on with whatever is next in his day without feeling guilty about anything, the parent wants the convenience of being able to walk along a clean street.

But again the best way to work through this is to understand the goal conflict, not to look at attributes. Can we make life more convenient for the dog owner (such as with a free supply of plastic bags) while playing up the guilty factor, such as with personalised notices from children about how much they dislike stepping in dog's mess? Can we aim for a street which is not completely clean, but clean enough?

A shipping paint job

And here's an illustration of a more complex organisational example where software might be involved. Consider a ship which needs a "paint job", going to a shipyard to have part of its paint coating renewed. The shipowner wants the shipyard which can provide an acceptable service at lowest price. There is a system of "request for quotes", where the shipowner may give information such as the area of steel to be painted, the thickness of paint required, if there is any touch-up or "spot" painting needed.

The shipyard will try to provide a quote based on this. The shipyard has other criteria to consider, such as when the space is available for a ship, perhaps how well past dealings with the shipowner went, particularly with the inevitable unanticipated problems. The shipowner will gather the quotes and make a selection.

Probably, both shipping company and shipyard will be using some kind of software tool, which attempts to harness all the relevant attributes into a digital system. But this can only work effectively if the systems have been set up with the right model, which a (non-software using) person might use. How much should the shipowner weight a yard where there is a long standing personal relationship, rather than just on price? Does the shipyard's software accurately calculate how much it will actually cost the shipyard to do the work?

Children online security

Here's another digital example – there are real concerns about children's online games being accessed by adults with malicious intent, who contact the children and perhaps ask them to send photographs or meet in person.

We have two parties with completely different sets of objects and goals, what the child wants, what the malicious adult wants. As a regulator, how can we possibly solve this problem?

We don't actually need alignment on the goals to make a map to solve the problem, we just need to know what the goals are to fit it together. We could recognise that both child and adult are seeking to make connections, just in a different way.

Our map would point out the various activities a malicious adult might make in order to achieve their goal of connections, such as asking for certain information, or asking a child to move to another online game which is less restrictive in what sort of communications it accepts. The fix would then be to scan the communications for these sorts of requests, or material which may be sent as a result of such a request, such as a photo.

Digital project managers

Our intended audience for this book is digital project managers, people who are given a responsibility of making these digital projects work.

Project managers usually begin with a brief stated in terms of objects. What the deliverable should be, what the timetable should be, what the costs should be constrained to. Their first level task is also object related, making schedules and assessing risks.

But from this point onwards, we advise that project managers should consider thinking about elements of the project, as far as possible, in terms of goals and activities towards that goal. The organisation has goals, any digital technology has its goals, the project to get the digital technology deployed and utilised has its goals. Then these activities can be drawn together in a map.

We should only use objects when it is absolutely clear to everybody what those objects mean and that is the easiest way to explain them. There is no argument about what a dollar is. But a "schedule" means something different, depending on if you are a scheduler or a participant in a complex schedule (such as an airline pilot). Similarly a "clean street" might be defined differently if you are a parent or a lazy dog owner.

We never want to be the manager who thinks that the data in his spreadsheet is more important than the work behind this data – although many of us have met such a manager. It is a lazy, and easy way of managing which omits the need to understand what is really going on.

Moving from objects to activities

People have seamlessly moved from objects to activities in their minds as long as people have been in organisations. A shipowner wants the ship painted (an object), and a contract with the shipyard (an object), but also understands that the yard will need to be able to engage in the activity of painting in a way which is safe and economically viable. The shipowner knows that the shipyard will have a number of different painting tasks to complete, and the schedule may need to change if a task takes longer than expected.

We could build a map of this, showing the main goals of the shipowner and shipyard, and the factors which influence them. Probably we would do this by talking to people who have actually done these roles on both sides and try to write down the mental maps which they already have.

Then the best digital technology we could make would emphasise these important parts of the transaction. That way, people would find it useful, because it tells them what they want to know. And the 'change management' transition to better software is much easier.

Think about how artists see the world – in an artist's mind, nothing is purely an object, even it actually is an object, such as a painting or a performance. We'll explore why this is later in this book.

SOME BASIC IDEAS BEHIND MAPS AND ACTIVITIES

I n this chapter we look at basic ideas behind our concept of maps and activities, including how it relates to the work of a digital project manager and a computer programmer, what the map looks like, the concept of abstraction levels, the link between maps and stories. We'll look at the link to "design thinking", ways to establish the scope of the map, and the importance of linking with goals.

The space between project manager and programmer

In a digital project, the project manager is responsible for getting the project delivered.

This person takes an abstracted (high level) view of what is happening. Maintaining a focus on where we are trying to go, and if we are on track to get there. Maintaining a focus on the main moving parts – such as the people involved, their motivation levels, the choice of technologies, the technology vendors. Whether the project can be done the same way as it was done in other parts of the world. The risks of something going wrong.

Meanwhile, the programmers' role could be defined as giving instructions to a computer to make it do what they want. This is what programming is. We must never forget that computers do not possess any innate intelligence, only the capability to follow a highly precise list of instructions, known as 'code' or 'algorithms'. It is the programmers' skill to create this.

It is the space between project managers, programmers, and others involved, such as the users, which has the potential to go wrong. It would be great if project managers could just define where the project should go, tell programmers, and they would get on and build it. But when the programmers find they do not have enough information to know what needs to be built, and so they need to figure a great deal out themselves, and they can't communicate this easily back to the project manager, the complexity level increases and things start going wrong.

The answer is more than just to say, there should be a map when previously there was not a map. Every project already has some kind of plan. What we are saying specifically is that the map making should be done with more granularity, more focus, and more competency – and we suggest some ways to get there. And perhaps it is the project managers' role to develop this competency and take on this role.

What is this map

This map, in itself, is nothing technical at all, and does not follow any prescribed format.

We can consider it like we would a conversation – a means for exchanging information between people.

There are no rules for how we should have a conversation. We all develop our own internal methods, different ways we communicate different information with different people around us, whether we are socializing, with family, or in a work meeting. And it would be the same with this sort of map.

Abstraction and granularisation levels

The most important concept in our idea of map making is of the 'abstraction level'.

Everything in life can be looked at, at varying levels of detail, which we call the "abstraction" level. Less detail means higher abstraction.

Abstracting is something we do if we were explaining our daily work to our parents or friends. In our head, we have a detailed picture of everything we need to do today, who we need to talk to, and what we are going to say. But if we explain it to someone else who does not understand our domain, we might explain in more abstract terms, saying we are building new software, working in a hospital or bank, or building a new manufacturing plant, and roughly what our role entails.

The opposite of abstracting is granularising. We can all do this too, every day. Imagine if we are explaining to a child how to do something routine for us, like wash up dishes. Or explaining to a builder how we want our new kitchen to be built. Or giving instructions to any service provider or business partner who will be looking at whatever we are doing in far more detail than we are, in order to deliver what we are looking for.

Teachers the world over have learned to convey complex ideas by breaking them down into simpler ones, and then build on them, a process involving a mixture of granularising and abstracting.

Sometimes in life we start with the granular detail and try to group things together to make a pathway. For example, when we are developing our mental 'models' of what usually work when our child has a tantrum, or if we are figuring out the best driving route. In business we often want to summarise what we are doing so someone else can easily understand it.

We can describe organisations in abstract or granular terms. For example we could describe a bank in abstract terms as an "organisation which takes and lends money and moves money around". We could describe it in low abstraction in terms of what the individuals specifically do all day and the steps they take, such as approving loans, ensuring financial transfers are carried out successfully, resolving customer problems.

If we were making a paper map for a certain goal, then we would do a continuous process of abstracting and granularising. We might start with an abstract reason we are making this map (for example, to help walkers, car drivers or property developers). We would survey detailed (granular) information about the land, and then abstract to pick which details we are going to present on the map. We might discover that the picture we are creating is no use for the intended purpose at all, and so change our surveying methods.

In a similar way, software map making involves a continuous process of abstracting and granularising. We start with a picture of what we want to build, we discuss it with people who will do the detailed work, they come up with reasons why it might not work, or problems we might not have thought about.

As project managers, we abstract and roll-up this information to try to work out if this is just going to be the sort of teething problems which every project comes across (and manages to overcome), or if it is a problem which will ruin our day. We update our 'abstracted' picture and then revise the granularised picture.

Maps come from stories

In life we often come across other people's mental maps. For example, when we read magazine articles about what celebrities like to do on weekends, or how an investor makes a certain decision, this could be considered a story of someone else's map.

Maps can be much easier to understand and absorb when they are presented as stories, rather than as visualisations. Stories about something which happened in the past, and so the reason we do something new. For example, you hear a story about how the government updated its methods for determining whether a suspected terrorist is released from jail, after someone was released from jail and went on to make a terrorist attack.

We often see maps as visualisations, too. A paper map is a visualisation. Some business presentations can be full of them. Understanding someone else's visualisation of their mental map can be very hard work, if you don't know the story behind it.

Connection with "design thinking"

The term "design thinking" is often heard in software circles. It can be defined as an iterative process to find a better way to solve a problem, rather than following a linear approach.

Design thinking is not usually defined any more specifically than that. If you train in a discipline which uses design thinking, such as architecture or graphic design, your training may involve a lot of projects which are then assessed. But you are not taught specifically how to find a solution.

Our software map making approach could be defined as a form of design thinking, in that a map could be considered a design. But we are trying to do more, suggest pointers and a structure about how a map should be created, rather than just say, try and build it and we'll assess it afterwards.

Not all 'design thinking' is map making.

The map's scope is limitless

An organisational map, and an organisational software map, can have a vast scope. We can extend the map outwards to cover everything that the organisation does, and extend it inwards to include every activity every individual does, and every piece of information.

Imagine what a map for the e-commerce company Amazon would look like. There would be a massive strategic part, a massive operational part, the work to continually improve websites, improve how warehouses operate, improve the choice of products on offer. The operational part would connect the online order to billing, packing in the warehouse, and delivery.

We don't need to build limitless maps. But the maps we do build probably should have a limited scope, if they are to be any use. For example, we could make a map for a specific digital technology implementation project. Or a map for a project to improve efficiency of a certain operation, or reduce the amount of money being spent on a certain input.

The organisational map, as a basis for digital technology, describes how the organisation functions. It does not need to get into 'higher level' elements such as why the company exists, and how it fundamentally makes value. It needs to focus on the day to day aspects of what a company does and how its activities lead towards its goals.

You need to know what is important when making a map. For example lunch breaks are probably not an important component of an office-based task, but can be a critical component in scheduling a lorry driver's rota, ensuring that regulations for rest periods are complied with.

Goal focused

The second core concept in our idea of map making is that the map should be organised around a specific goal and the activities to get there. This goal can be anything the company wishes to achieve, such as to implement a specific software tool, or build an automation system, or to improve efficiency or safety.

The critical point here is that the map should not be constructed around non-goal elements (which we call objects), such as having a schedule or spending time writing code. The reason is that goal-based activities can be easily abstracted or granularised, while objects become something different when looked at from another abstraction level.

Here's an illustration of that idea. Let's try describing a project using objects. The project manager is refining a work schedule (an object). The work schedule includes various tasks, such as creating and testing code, and running trials with the people who will work with it. There are tasks (another object) given to a programmer, who will spend time coding (another object). The coding is more complicated than expected, so takes longer, and the schedule is completely wrong.

The complication level of the coding task, and the adherence to the project schedule, are related, but not in an obvious way.

If we take the same discussion in terms of activities, we might say the project manager is assessing what activities are required to achieve the goal, and how long they will take. The map shows a detailed picture of the activities, what exactly needs to be done, what the risks might be. The map gradually breaks down the activities into small pieces of activity, with a clear idea of what each small piece involves. So it gets easier to get a clear view of how long each activity will take, and so make a more reliable schedule.

Our purpose and goal here

Now we have talked about goals, it seems a good time to explain the goal of this book.

We want to encourage you, as a project manager, to think more about map making as part of enterprise digital projects.

We want to help you see how you can do it more easily, based on what other people have done and thought through, rather than to try to persuade.

The number of different maps that could be drawn for organisations and software projects is about as many as the number of different types of organisations and projects there are. All maps are different. It would not – we think – be possible to produce a guide to show you exactly how to make any kind of map.

But there are key techniques, goals and technologies which will help with map making, and this is what we write about in this book.

We will support discussions with project managers and domain experts to share what you have already done in terms of maps, how those maps worked and what they did.

We hope to continue this work with a series of events and publications, gathering experiences from others, to build a body of knowledge about better ways to make enterprise digital technology maps.

INTRODUCTION TO MAP MAKING TECHNIQUES

Maps at the start of the project

It is important to have someone capable of building maps involved in projects right from the start.

We hear that too often, map making skills are brought in too late. Businesses make a decision to embark on a project, and then realise after they have started the work that it is much more complicated than they expected.

This probably mean that whoever starts the project off should be involved in the map making – such as the person in the executive suite. Then the work can be carried out by the program manager or project manager.

Lines and nodes

One way to start thinking a map could be with 'lines and nodes. A node is a critical thing. The lines are the factors affecting that thing.

A line and node map might be described more easily in words than by actually drawing one.

To explain with a simple example, let's say your goal is to replenish your family food supplies. The critical task in achieving this goal is a visit to a supermarket.

There are various activities you might do before going to the supermarket, such as checking to see what you have in your fridge, asking other family members if they want anything, making a plan to visit a grocery shop which fits with other activities you have that day, and making a plan to bring the groceries home quickly afterwards.

There are 'risks' involved, such as that the shop does not have everything you need, so you would decide whether to get an alternative, not to bother, or go to a different shop.

All of this might be drawn as a central 'node' of the grocery shop visit, surrounded by lines indicating the other factors.

This activity will also integrate with other activities, such as making family dinner, making a packed lunch, planning your next few days, and earning money to pay for the food.

This example is chosen as being something simple enough that you can visualize the map with lines and nodes – but the real life examples from work will be much more complicated, if we are planning the construction of a building, a software implementation, an efficiency improvement in a hospital department, a way to improve efficiency of a ship engine. There will be many more people involved, all with their own activities linking with ours, and more critical 'nodes', such as things we really want to avoid.

The core node can be whatever is important in this activity. In a business project, the important thing might be to change a certain key performance indicator (KPI), in which case the KPI would be the core node, and the lines to other nodes represent the factors which drive this KPI.

For example, if it is a project to reduce average waiting times in the emergency department of a hospital. The 'node' is the KPI and the lines linked to this node are factors which drive it, such as a shortage of staff at times of high patient entry in a cold winter.

An important task in map making is understanding the process dependencies, where the outcome of one task (such as recruitment of nurses in the above case) becomes an input to another, or affects another.

Some activity models are more demanding

In our working environments, people in different roles have different levels of complexity in their activity models.

More junior roles will typically have simpler activity models. The more complex the activity model, the more demanding it is on the person, the greater the person's mental 'bandwidth' required to keep on top of it, the more skills and experience are needed.

Larger organisations can develop their own complexity because each individual may have to work with many other individuals, and there are more requirements of the work.

So the activity of being a street cleaner, working for a council organisation, can be more complex than the activity of cleaning your own house. But the activity of managing the regions street cleaning services is more complex still.

Anyone in a staff 'oversight' role is monitoring the activities of all the staff, as well as connecting to a bigger picture, if the overall organisation is fulfilling its function and what is demanded of it.

The map making rarely starts from scratch

Companies rarely embark on a completely new map making process. It is more likely that they will start with the map they used when they did the same project last time, but add in extra elements to get a better understanding (and leave less for the people doing the granular work to figure out themselves).

Consider a company which builds hydroelectric dams. It will probably have built a number of dams over the past decades, and have a reasonably good idea how to do it. It may have found one of the biggest problems with the last project was poor relationship with local communities, which led to protests and the project being delayed.

So it will revise and add more granularity to the map, to say perhaps that it will hold local meetings right from the start of the process, and not take it for granted that local acceptance will be achieved, and gradually develop the way it works with local people.

Past experience will teach what the biggest risks and hazards are – such as a previous project which overran in time and cost, what the causes are, and how to prevent it next time.

Similarly, not all software projects in organisations are 'greenfield' – making new software.

In the real world, software project managers might be involved in tasks like assessing whether it would be good to update old software, and making a map of what exactly this old software does.

We hear that many banks still have software tools which are decades old.

Digital technology in different

abstraction levels

Here's an example of how a company might look at a digital technology project at different abstraction / granularity levels, starting with high abstraction / low granularity.

Level 1 = What does the organisation do to fundamentally make value? How does the organisation and its customers operate from day to day, described in abstracted form? What does digital technology offer which may assist with its work to make value? What is the master digital transformation strategy – what are we trying to change?

Level 2 = What is the current status with the digital technology we use? What new digital tools do we need to implement to take us to the place we want to go?

Level 3 = What will our process be of implementing various new digital tools, and assessing if they are working?

Level 4 = What digital tools exactly do we need to implement? Can we buy it, or do we need to build it ourselves?. How will we assess them? What specific tasks are people doing, what information do they need to do them better, where can computers help them do better?

Level 5 = what are the specific requirements for the digital tools we are going to create in-house?

Activity models

At the granular end of the map, there might be activity models. What are people doing, what do they need to support them.

If it is a software project, the activity model might include what information the software needs to provide to them, or how the analytic capability of the software will fit with what they are doing.

Every organisation involves activities, unless it does not employ people at all. If it is a bank, the activity might be for customers to file a mortgage application, and the bank to have a process of deciding whether or not it is accepted. If it is a cement factory, the activity might be for people who monitor the overall operations. The operations may be automated, but people have roles of overseeing what is happening and spotting problems.

If it is a hospital, the patients have their own 'activity' as they are moved through the various processes of an operation, childbirth or something else. The staff have their own activities.

The above shows that the range of activities people do in and around a working environment is enormously diverse. Some activities could be defined easily with a spreadsheet or Gantt chart, others cannot be.

But all of the activities can be understood by people doing them, and written down in words, as we are doing here – if they could not be, then they could not be done by people. And this means they can be included in a map.

So we cannot prescribe exactly what an activity map looks like, just say that it can probably be drawn for any human activity which has any kind of structure to it.

Continually improving the map

Another core function of the map is that it can be continually improved.

If the map is purely mental (held in people's heads), then it can be improved as easily as we can update the understanding we have in our heads. This is a capability we all have as part of our normal work. We see things have changed and update our picture.

If the map has any physical form, such as a written document or computer visualisation, that increases rigidity, in that creates a work process for updating the map – such as issuing a new version of the document. But it should still be much easier to update the map than update the real-world elements the map relates to.

Companies rarely know exactly how to get to where they want to go, and so the map is likely to need multiple iterations.

Mental maps or written down?

Organisations have a mixture of mental maps and written down maps.

Consider a hazardous working environment, such as a ship, where all the working procedures are written down. The company figures out how to do various activities in a way which minimises risk, and demands that its staff follow them rigidly.

A trading environment, by contrast, relies on people using their instincts and making fast decisions. There will be processes written down, but not processes on the core activity of deciding how to trade. Individuals develop their mental maps of what works and what doesn't with trading, and continually improve them as they see what has worked.

Persistence of process

A common theme of problems in organisations is a mismatch between how people doing the actual activity see the world, and how senior managers or project managers see the world.

Think about complaints from doctors that the hospital management have no understanding of what it is like to be a doctor, or any complaint that the leaders are 'out of touch'.

The map making process can bridge this connection by creating a view of the world which people can work with at both ends of the scale. So at the same time, you can see the details of front-line day to day work, and do 'roll-up' management, working out if any big changes need to be made.

We can call this 'persistence of process'. How well do the ideas of the process 'persist' up the chain, from the front-end view to the abstracted view?

Can the leaders and project managers, who need the abstracted view, easily keep a track of what they are looking at, which aligns with how people doing the front-end work see it?

This problem can be cofounded if there are any obstacles to communication, such as data at the front-end level which needs to be treated as confidential, or information which people are not sharing.

Human minds mix activities and objects - computers don't

In our lives, we have a mind boggling array of activities and goals. It isn't mind boggling to do it, because our minds have evolved to do it. But it is mind boggling to start to think about how it works.

Consider retail. Many people want beautiful bodies. That is fundamentally an activity, some mixture of diet, exercise. Let's say the activity of spending part of the day being hungry in order to not eat too much, and doing some physical activity, in pursuit of this goal. (Also aging, which is an activity, but not one we have much control over).

Instead of this activity, we see a beautiful body as an object. We seek to purchase objects which will connect us to this desired object. We fail to see that buying for example a certain piece of clothing will not make us beautiful. Objects do not connect together in the way that activities do.

Then we go shopping, which is an activity towards this goal of purchasing objects. A completely different activity to the one needed to be beautiful and a goal which does not relate. Yet somehow, it does.

Many people have attempted to bring computing to retail. But computers have no understanding of any of this. The most the computer can do is spot patterns in people's activity and guess they may relate to other people's activity. This can be useful but could also be compared to trying to understand how a society operates without being part of it - very limited in what it can do.

Here's another example. The gift of musicians could be described as bringing a sense of activity to a place where there previously was no sense of activity, just objects. The activity itself is sometimes indescribable, and sometimes it can be described, but in very human terms, such as re–affirming our belief that life is fundamentally good, or works in the way we would like to believe that it does.

Musicians do actually produce objects - such as songs or performances. People buy or listen to these objects and see them very differently to the person who created them. But somehow the activity relates - when a musician creates a work which can create a sense of activity, it can resonate with the listener, so they also feel the same sense of activity, which they like.

A third example is the way we mature as individuals. When we are younger, everything is an activity to a goal - either to be entertained or interested, or to satisfy our basic needs. When we start our working lives, we have career goals. As we get older, our interest in career goals declines, and life becomes more a series of objects - waking, eating, dressing, doing the list of tasks we do.

A fourth example is the misunderstanding of the capability of autonomous cars. Driving involves objects - the road, the vehicle, other vehicles, other elements in the road. It also involves goals - our own goal usually to get to our destination reasonably quickly and safely while not being too rude to other road users. We understand other road users probably have the same goal (but not necessarily). And we understand how the various parameters play out differently in the mind of a young car driver, an older car driver, a cyclist, a bus driver, a van driver, a pedestrian. We put all this together in our minds with no problem.

A computer system can just about work out how to achieve its own goal, reducing it to a set of objects. But it can't go so far as to interact with anyone else's goal. It can only understand objects, not goals.

So autonomous driving may master the 'object' part of driving - keeping on the road, not hitting anything provided it has time to brake. But it will never understand the "activities to goals" part of any other road user.

In the software world, software is an object, but it is also something built around a certain person's view of the world, how they put together objects to form an activity to achieve their goal. Another piece of software will be put together around objects for someone else's goal. Like the example we mentioned about the shipyard's software system for generating quotes with the shipping company customer's procurement system. When these systems are purely built around objects, not activities, they will never integrate, and it would be foolish to try.

Making the map consistent

If someone has worked out how something works in their mind, they can easily build a map of it. Because the map is essentially the same as we think of things in our mind. What are the important elements and what connects to these.

But if the map is used as a basis for project development work, we need to make it consistent and understandable.

We should also be clear if we are talking about objects or activities. Many objects can be both - it can depend how they are being used.

For example, the condition of a piece of equipment can be recorded as a status for the benefit of software calculating for example that poor condition equipment must be replaced. It could be used to make a schedule of maintenance work.

But if we are making a judgement of the condition of equipment, and whether it needs to be replaced, we know that it has been flagged in a system as "in poor condition" is just a starting point not an end point. Perhaps the system really needs to be retired, or perhaps it just needs ten minute work by someone with moderate skill to get it back into condition again.

In the human brain, we can happily mix up objects and activities, as we do with basic activities in our daily life, or at work, when we can be making something one second and treating it as an object another.

But computers cannot mix up objects and activities, and cannot understand activities and goals at all. They can only understand objects.

The same for our maps. We need to be consistent about whether something is seen as an object or an activity, not change partway through.

We should probably only use objects at all if it is clear (no ambiguity) to everybody what they mean.

Karl Jeffery + Dimitris Lyras

THE ROLE OF THE PROJECT MANAGER

Project managers have had an important role in organisations for decades, but are relatively new to the world of digital technology.

The project management skillset might be described as someone who keeps mentally on top of the big issues of a project – what it will do, the costs, the timetable, the people involved- so they know what to do to deliver this.

If the project is too complicated for one person to hold all the details in their head – as nearly all big projects are – then the project manager needs to be selective as to what details to keep on top of. They will probably need a large mental bandwidth to hold a lot of moving details.

The project manager will also need a focus on the goal of the project – what is to be built, and at what budget – and capable of assessing how changes at a detailed level will affect the overall goal.

In the construction world (physical buildings), the project manager discipline came about in the mid-20th century. Before that, construction might have been led by architects or engineers – technical people.

They probably found that purely technical people can be the wrong people to run projects effectively, if they are more interested in technical advances than in making sure the project delivers.

In a similar way, a software development team who are mainly interested in finding new ways to use artificial intelligence, rather than making software which helps their customer achieve its goals.

The idea of the project manager has passed to the digital technology world, as companies have discovered there are benefits to digital technology projects being led by someone with project management expertise.

Our proposal is that the software mapmaking role, we describe here, could either be an extension of the project managers' role, or held by someone working closely with the project manager.

Map making does require capability to think conceptually.

All projects involve some level of conceptual thinking, e.g. reading between the lines of the information available to judge if a project is on track. So this is part of the project manager's skillset, but is perhaps not a core part of it.

Linear vs conceptual thinking

A linear thinking person, which may be thought of as "left brain", distils work into a series of linear steps. This happens, then this happens, and if everyone does their job properly the end result is good.

Linear thinking is fine for complex projects where everything can be seen as a series of steps, such as developing a new oil field, constructing a hospital, constructing a coffee shop which looks the same as the last one, hiring a team of people who can do the required work.

Linear thinkers might see life in terms of a competition – who can develop the best linear structure for a project, and then ensure that the line is adhered to by everyone involved. Linear thinkers are more likely to think of the elements of the project in terms of objects.

Conceptual thinking, which can be thought of as 'right brain', could be described as floating around different ideas in your brain until you come up with a structure, or map, which works, delivering the desired result with the available resources. We typically think of artists as ultimate conceptual thinkers, although not all conceptual thinking is art.

This sort of thinking is required for any project where the pathway is not immediately apparent, and we can't rely on our first idea for how to get there. Projects where we need more complex map making.

In projects, conceptual thinkers tend to be better at seeing the various elements of the project as goals and activities, rather than objects, seeing everything in the context of whether it helps the organisation achieve its goal.

Conceptual people can take less of a competitive view of life – they recognize that it can take multiple people to develop good concepts or maps, and more input can make the map better.

Most people are not extreme linear or conceptual thinkers, they come some way between two extremes, and have capability to do both.

Linear thinkers can run into problems with map making if they cannot see the elements in terms of goals and activities to achieve the goals, only as objects. Or if they think that the first linear sequence they develop is fine. Or if they think that linear thinking is the only mindset which works in this environment, and get frustrated by having to work with conceptual thinkers. Or if they are less comfortable with the more collaborative nature of map making.

Many people in senior roles at organisations are linear thinkers. Most organisations are, in their core, doing a technical or operational activity, and so have recruited technical people. People self-select themselves as being either 'technical' or 'creative' people in our school education systems. Companies often promote linear thinkers over conceptual thinkers, because they might have better capability in technical or operational roles.

Encouraging conceptual thinking

So the challenge at the heart of this book might be described as encouraging project managers, often linear thinkers, to think more conceptually.

Imagine a school art teacher, gently encouraging people to be creative, who do not usually think in creative terms.

There is a lot of fear involved with conceptual work – as with any art – because it involves creating something which has never been done, and may never work. All creative people feel fear, and the successful creative people are those who learn ways to tackle their fear and stop it impeding their work.

Linear people will feel fear at the idea of a conceptual project – and perhaps this fear is what has driven them to more linear work. The challenge here might be described as encouraging them to overcome this fear.

Transforming the organisation

The ultimate goal of a digital project is usually to transform how the organisation works, not just to make and implement new technology or tools. To put it another way, it is totally possible to develop great tools but find that the organisation cannot be persuaded to use them.

And much of the work of the project manager might be in changing the organisation so it is more capable of adopting new tools.

HOW MAP MAKING HELPS WITH A PROJECT MANAGER'S TASKS

I n this chapter, we look at the key parts of a project manager's core role, and how map making can help. Such as defining scope for the project, making timetables and budgets, putting together a group of employees and vendors to deliver it, and leading them to deliver the project, while keeping on top of the risks and regional variances.

Planning and defining scope

The key role of the project manager is deciding where the project is going at a top level. Or this may have been decided by the company executives or program manager before the project manager got involved.

The scope would be decided before the map making process begins, otherwise you don't know what the map is for.

But as the map evolves, the scope may also evolve – it will certainly gain more definition, becoming more of a realistic plan, as the map making process identifies parts of the original plan which look unworkable.

This can be a two-way iteration. We start with a rough idea where we are going and how to get there, make maps, connect to people who are going to do the granular work and then update the map, leading to an updated scope.

Consider how we might come up with a plan for a house, and then have to refine our plan to be much more realistic after a talk to the builder or working out the practicalities and costs. We might find that our overall scope breaks down into many sub projects, and have to cut the number of sub projects down.

Making executable plans

The plan becomes 'executable' once the map has enough granularity in it to give adequate information to the people doing the actual building, implementing and executing, to tell them exactly what they want to do – and you know in advance that it will work. In other words, executable plans are a result of an adequate map.

Working with vendors

Vendors are people who implement part of the plan, paid a fee rather than employed. An adequate map will show vendors exactly what to do, in the same way as a good building plan gives precise instructions to the builders.

If the vendor is a software company, they may have already built software according to a map which is different to yours, and encourage you to use it, since that is much cheaper for them.

Vendors may have an incentive to want to take control of a part of the map, effectively running part of the project for you. You need to be very careful about that, because their incentives are not necessarily aligned with yours (as a project manager).

Time estimating, cost and resource estimating

The better the map is, the better information it will feed up to the project manager about how much time and resource will be required to implement the plan.

The map may not explicitly include information about costs and time required, but it can include information about the tasks, what is involved in doing them, and who will do them. This is the input information you need to work out how much they will cost and how long they will take, and so plan out timing, costs and schedule for the whole project.

Project risk analysis: including

cybersecurity risks

A good map should make the risks clearer. If it is a digital technology project, typical risks might include a project taking much longer to build than expected, or encountering obstacles which had not been predicted, or problems with software systems not interoperating as well as expected.

There are already structured mapping approaches developed for operational risks, such as the "Hazop" process, where you study what may go wrong, what factors may lead to that happening, and what processes are in place to fix the problem were it to emerge, before it gets much worse.

Using Agile as part of project management

The Agile process is a structured way to iterate. You have a team which puts intense focus into something for a period of time such as 2 weeks, then evaluates the results, and only continues if there is evidence of progress. So it is good for projects where you don't have a clear idea what is required or if it will work, so you do not waste time doing something which does not work and keep re-evaluating.

There are many projects in the digital domain where it is hard to have a clear idea where you are going. You might be working with old data without a clear idea of how easy the data will be to understand. You might be making tools for people without a clear idea of whether they will want to use them, or find them helpful, or how much persuading it will take.

Creating documentation

The map itself can generate the documentation. For example, as in the costing example, if the document is about the costs, you can use the information in the map to get information about the activities involved in the processes, and so work out how long they will take and how much they will cost.

If the documentation is about specific work to be done by a programmer, the map can provide the information needed for this.

If the documentation is an update for the company board about the progress so far and key risks, the map should help generate this.

Team leadership

Team leadership could be defined as being able to guide individuals as to what they need to do, and spotting when they are going off track. It is possible that less skilled and accountable people will make mistakes.

There are elements of leadership which have nothing to do with map making, such as personal skills and charisma. But there are elements of leadership which are very much linked to map making – such as the ability to quickly spot whether or not something is on track, or what is needed to be done to fix it.

Strategic influencing

Strategic influencing could be defined as getting people at both ends of the map to do what you want.

People at the 'execution' end – such as domain experts and programmers – are more open to being influenced if they understand what is expected of them, it fits with their pre-existing mental model of the world and their work in it. The more detail the map provides, the easier this should be.

People at the "C suite" end of the map should be more open to being influenced if they can be shown more clearly why they need to change their views about how something should be developed. A map can show more clearly where the problems are with the current plan and why it may need to be changed.

Making a global project or portfolio

If you are implementing the same system in multiple parts of the world, you want to know about reasons the implementation may turn out differently in different places. There can be different culture, regulation, market, attitudes to change.

The map should help identify these. It will distil the work into specific sub activities. Someone who knows the local environment well should be able to see which of the sub-activities will work or not work in that part of the world.

If there are major differences, such as a different regulation or requirement to use a certain supplier, this may lead to an adjustment of part of the map. But your map making process can let you see more clearly what parts you need to change, and which parts can stay as they are.

Consider if you have visited a restaurant, coffee shop or hotel chain in different countries, like Starbucks or McDonalds. Some aspects will be identical, but not all of them – there are small changes in the menu, seating layout, store design, as the business has worked out elements of its central operational 'map' it needed to change to match local requirements and differences.

TECHNOLOGIES AND TECHNOLOGICAL APPROACHES

I n this section we look at technologies and technological approaches which will commonly come up in map making, including a choice of buying or building software, tools to help build maps, Agile, cybersecurity maps, robotic process automation, and advanced technologies like AI

Software – buy or build?

Any digital projects might involve decisions about whether to use off the shelf software, or how.

This decision ought to fit into the map making process.

We need to be aware, from the outset, that off the shelf software has been designed for processes different to ours. Perhaps it was custom made for one client, and the vendor wants to try selling it to another. Perhaps the software has multiple functionality, so it has the potential to do whatever anybody wants, but there is enormous effort needed to get it working.

Perhaps the software does not quite fit with our map, but it fits closely enough that it would be better for us to use it than make our own. But then we might need to change our map so that it works with the software.

And of course if we buy software ready-made, it will probably be cheaper, and the software company should keep updating it.

These are not easy decisions to make. But the clearer an understanding we have of what digital technology we want, obtained through the map making process, should help.

Software map making tools

The project management world is one of tools. We have visual tools, such as the Gantt chart, which shows the timeline of the project and when different elements will happen. There are software tools, to keep track of various major elements of a project, such as the contracts, or the status of construction.

There are also various software modelling tools. One of the first which comes to mind us Universal Modelling Language (UML). Although this is maybe not so useful for the sort of mapping we are talking about here, because it is geared towards objects, such as rows in a database or physical artefacts, not goals.

There have been modelling tools developed to track the flow of information in an organisation.

This is a new field – there may be good software mapping tools we haven't discovered yet. Also it would be a shame if software mapping tools restricted us to doing the mapping in a certain way, when we found another is better.

Software which automates map making

There have been software tools on offer which promise to automate a large part of the map making process within their software.

This includes software tools which promise to make accurate estimations of the cost of developing new software, and software tools which promise to automate the process of making apps.

In other words, rather than make the map yourself, you can just buy it, or have it made automatically for you.

This seems like a very ambitious promise for a software application to make. Obviously real-life applications will vary, but it seems very difficult to program a computer to make a calculation of how much it will cost to build a new software application, which could be anything from a few lines of code to a new version of Windows Operating system.

It is very hard to assess the complexity of anything before you start.

Agile working methods

Agile methods are popular as a means of working in way which is both structured and iterative. You try building something, and if it doesn't work, toss it away and try something different. But you try hard to make it work over a limited period of time.

Agile work can be an important part of map-driven processes. In theory, if the map is accurate and comprehensive enough, it should be possible to get the work right the first time you try it. That's like saying if you have a good road map of how to drive across the country, you should get there the first time you try.

But in real life we are going to places nobody has been before, building software which no-one has built before. So that's more equivalent to finding a method and route of getting to the South Pole in 1914. We may discover that, despite all our planning, we don't have a valid means of getting there, and need to change direction or approach before it gets too late.

Agile in organisations is not about dropping structure entirely. Companies working with agile will typically have closely agreed plans of where they are going to go, and their rough method of getting there. This is all part of the organisational map.

So perhaps the right way to place Agile in this discussion could be for the places where we don't have enough information to understand where we are going and how to get there in advance. And we never have all the information we need.

Cybersecurity maps

Cybersecurity needs to be thought of at the same time as any software project. Security requirements are getting more complex and that trend will probably continue.

Cybersecurity throws up a diverse range of problems, such as managing the logons to the system (and managing the person who manages the logons), managing integrity of certain data (so it cannot be corrupted or accessed by someone who is not authorised), and training staff so they are aware of risks, such of other people trying to gain access to their systems or logons.

Cybersecurity is a real-world problem which may be better solved with a map making approach than how it is usually approached, just by erecting more barriers.

Erecting barriers sounds like a sensible response to a cybersecurity threat - if someone guessed your password, make passwords harder to guess. But - as we all know from practical experience - cyber security methods can also make digital technology unworkable, when the same barriers obstruct us from doing our work.

So cyber security would actually benefit much more from map making - so we can make systems which are simultaneously secure and easy to use.

As we see in the real world, it is totally possible to have high security without obstruction. The method of locks and keys is adequate for nearly all of us to protect our houses and families while we sleep, while causing very little disruption.

Managing computer logons is not a trivial exercise, particularly when it involves different layers of parties - someone to manage the logins for an organisation, who must themselves have authorisation managed - and a need to keep passwords themselves secret from everyone apart from the people who use them. But it can be done.

Robotic process automation

Robotic Process Automation (RPA) is about a computer doing elements of someone's administrative job. So to get value from RPA you need to think deeply about what aspects are involved in the actual person's job which you could train a computer to do, bearing mind that training computers is very expensive, or conversely it is much easier to train a computer to do something if it is extremely simple.

For example, a bank may be employing people who assess a company's suitability for credit. They do this by bringing up information about this company from various sources - company internal records, credit checks on the company and leading individuals, searches on the internet for bad news, any information about legal charges. These might be rigidly structured steps, which you could program a computer to do, taking the place of the person, including having its own logins to the various services.

But if your company's administrative staff spend most of their time doing a range of unstructured tasks, like responding to different queries, looking something up, changing someone's record, and this work involves some level of judgement / common sense (so can't be easily described so a computer could understand it), it is less of a candidate for Robotic Process Automation.

If you have a map of what the person's job is actually like, or a specific task they regularly do as a certain part of their job, and how many people in the organisation do the same thing, and an idea of how much it will cost to buy and set up the RPA, you can get a sense of whether it would be a good move and how to set about it.

The user interface

Digitalisation is also the art of getting the right information on a screen in front of somebody. Doing that requires understanding what someone needs to see at what time, filtering out information so they don't get overloaded, and then delivering that information to them so it is trustworthy and not accessed by the wrong people along the way.

But it is far more than the art of the user interface, because the screen display is just the tip of an iceberg of a complex system of gathering, processing and moving about information. It is just the end result – and determines whether or not the overall system works. All the talk about user interfaces may just be a distraction from the real work of understanding what people need to see and giving it to them.

For people to work with digital data, you ultimately need the right information in front of the right person – information at the time of need, visualised in a way they can work with it, filtered to avoid information overload, and trustworthy. To get to that point, you need to work out what someone needs at which time, work out how to present it, and work out how to get that information to them reliably and so it cannot be accessed or tampered by the wrong people along the way. Then what technology you need to buy or build to achieve that, and how it should be put together – including buy or build decisions.

Data analytics and AI

Many people thinking of software in 2020 think we must be talking about some advanced analytics or artificial intelligence / machine learning technique.

Our approach is that data analytics and AI can be part of enterprise software, they are a component, not the main thing.

The most important role of digital technology in any enterprise is to support the activities of that enterprise. That will involve some combination of products, suppliers, processes, activities, tasks, people and resources.

The company's achievement of its goals comes down to how well the organisation functions at its tasks and sub-tasks – which comes down to how well managed they are, whether the decision makers have the information they need, and so on.

If AI and analytics is used, it will probably be some component of a small part of an element here. A hospital employing radiographers using AI for image analysis. A car with some autonomous driving capability. Some robotic process automation, with a computer automatically doing administrative tasks which are simple and repetitive enough to describe to a computer.

Many companies use analytics for much broader decision making, such as a supermarket making a decision of how much of a certain good to order, based on consumption patterns in the past. We can call this 'operationalising' analytics. The computation involved will probably be more basic statistics, rather than any machine learning.

Many people have shared a vision of the whole company being driven by AI, but others, including AI experts, have stressed that this is only possible when – as a starting point – the organisation is fully digitised, all of it working processes are as digital as possible, and the data is in a form where people can easily work with it.

If the ultimate role of map making is to enable the main decision makers and project managers to make better decisions, bear in mind that will often involve trade-offs between different factors. These are complex decisions with multiple pieces of data involved. We are many years off from any AI system having this sort of capability.

It would probably be helpful for a digital project manager to have good expertise on advanced technologies, to be in a position to better understand whether a certain technology might help a company achieve its goal. There can be a wide gulf between the promises made about technology and what it can actually achieve in a working environment.

Low code

Project managers may do well to keep up to date with "low code" technologies – which are basically software tools for building software.

In theory, you feed your map into the low code software and it generates the software for you. So it can shorten the effort and cost between having a map and having software built according to the map.

Real life is not so simple, and perhaps this will only work with a very simple map, but the limitations are not obvious, and the technology is improving all the time.

Training and soft skills

Training and soft skills have a big part to play in all elements of map making and working with digital technology.

Do the project managers have the necessary skills to think conceptually about how to make a map, and let it continually improve over time, including 'soft skills' of working together with other stakeholders?

Can programmers take their instructions from a map, and supress any urge to invent things themselves?

And – perhaps most interesting – what role can better modelled software play in helping people learn – if it can give people at all levels a much better situation awareness of what is going on? Can the same software be used for training?

MAP MAKING MAKES LIFE GO BETTER

O rganisations with a more sophisticated map are better at giving us what we want, without letting us down or overwhelming us with complexity. They are better at having a managed process of continuous improvement, improving how they do activities in service of their goals.

An effective organisation means that, as a customer, we get the products we want inexpensively. As a citizen (or 'customer' of the state) we get easy to use systems for paying tax, accessing healthcare. We get education and transport services which work well for us. Any crime and justice issues to be handled properly.

If we have a disability, or a family member with one, we expect services to provide appropriate support. We expect a life of low risk. As an employee, we expect to be paid on time, while working suitable working hours, with suitable rest periods and holidays, in a safe working environment.

It was not like this in the past – where we had state systems which were brutal or non-existent. No education, healthcare, support if we are unemployed, no fair justice, and people resolved their differences with physical fights, leading in scale to warfare. Governments used fear and tyranny to collect taxes and obtain compliance. Survival was much more about luck.

The point here is not to show that life is better now, but to show that our organisations continue to be in a journey of improvement, to be even better modelled around what people need. A good organisation is not 'one size fits all', it is 'we have something to fit around everyone's individual needs'. The more comprehensive the mapping, the better this can be.

Conversely, when we feel let down by any organisation, either because it does not give us what we need or has too much bureaucracy, we can say that we are let down by its map making.

We can observe that the failure of map making happens to the people with the least resources – the poor or otherwise disadvantaged. So map making could be defined as trying to make the organisation run more efficiently, so it can serve less highly paying customers as well as the highly paying ones.

If there are enough resources, or a customer who is spends enough money, it is possible for people in the organisation to be paid to get around the weaknesses in our systems.

This is how, for example, luxury hotels can always offer good service - they are ultimately dependent on skilled people, not systems, and the people can overrule the systems. This is perhaps why the wealthier and more powerful among us do not usually perceive object based thinking to be a problem.

In other words, map making can make a complex organisation less complex.

Better maps can lead to better software – which can provide people with better situation awareness, so they can make better decisions and continually learn – while taking simpler tasks out of their hands via automation.

Regulation is a form of map making. A society can make rules such as the speed you can drive your car, when individuals can be released from jail, what healthcare services are available to certain people.

But regulation is a pretty rigid way to do something. The same rules apply to everyone, and everyone is different. If you are a regulator this is the only tool you have.

A map can offer a much more fluid way to manage organisations – meaning that different inputs lead to different outcomes or obligations. Maps can be more adaptable to changing risks, cause/effect relationships, and new knowledge.

We envisage that organisations will make increasingly big call for digital technology map makers, as projects get more complex.

If you enjoyed what you read in this book, and have some basic understanding of project management and digital technology, this could be a vocation for you.

But it can only work if we learn to see how our organisations operate in terms of activities towards goals, not just as objects. People have thought about the workings of organisations as objects for some time now - and also many of the individuals within them think that way.

With just object based thinking, there is a limit to how effective our organisations can ever become, and how good our systems can be.

This may be a real obstacle to the ideas in this book taking hold - and a reason they may never go anywhere.